Divide AND Ride

It's Carnival Day today
for our group of 11 best friends.

The Dare-Devil's first, and we'll need to divide.
2 people fit in each seat,
and each seat must be filled before we can ride.

We can fill 5 seats,
but 1 friend is left over
from our group of 11 best friends.

11 divided by 2 = 5 full seats

. . .with 1 friend left over.

Amanda yells, "Come and fill this seat!"
to a child we don't even know.

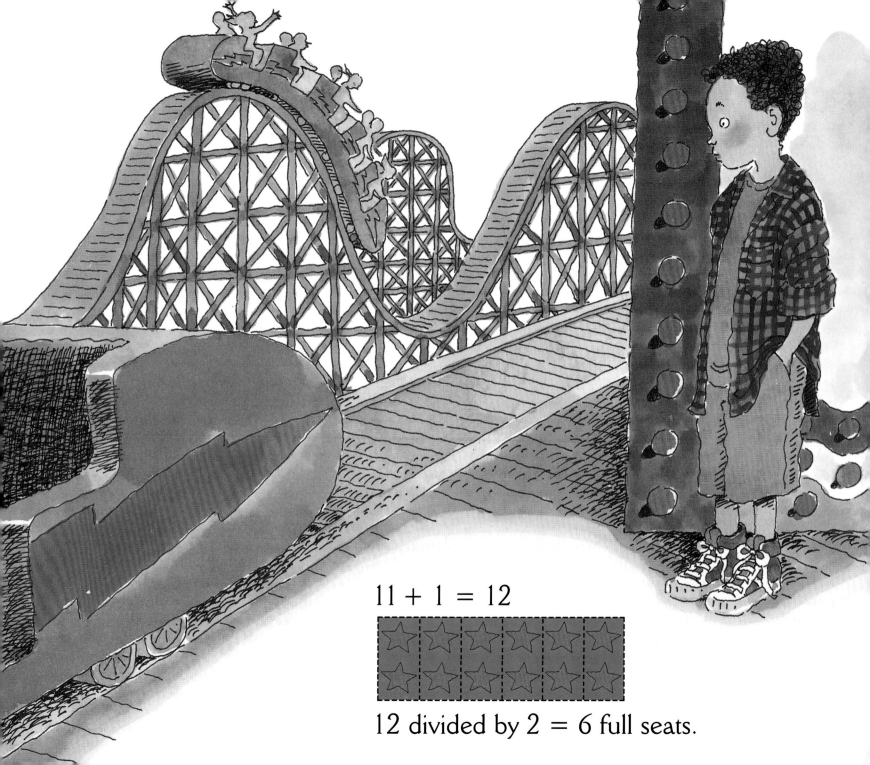

11 + 1 = 12

12 divided by 2 = 6 full seats.

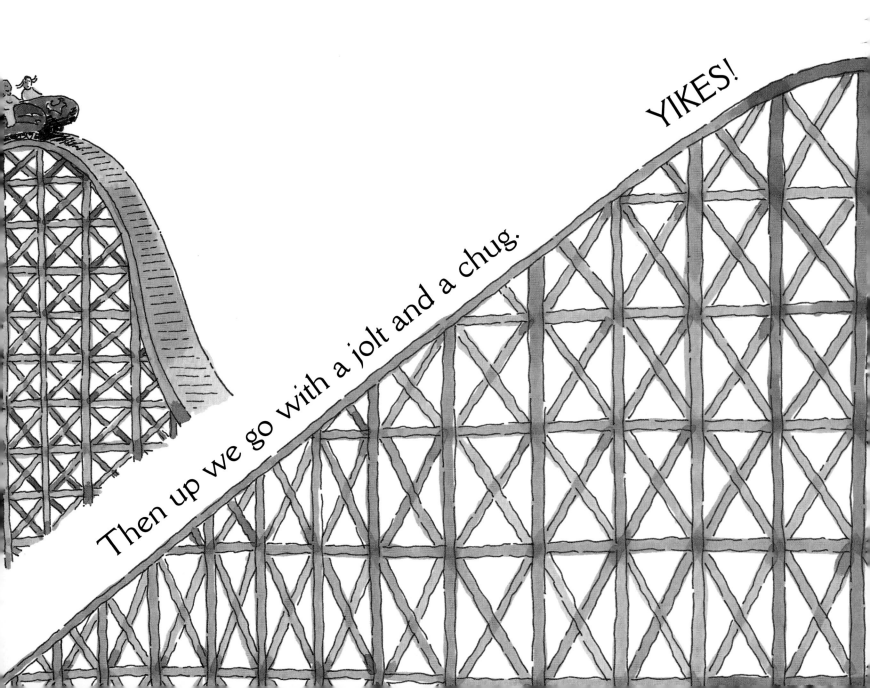

We're flying straight down!

For the Satellite Wheel,
again we'll divide.

It holds 3 people per chair,
and each chair must have 3
before we can ride.

We can fill 3 chairs,
but 2 friends are left over
from our group of 11 best friends.

11 divided by 3 = 3 full chairs

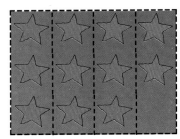

. . . .with 2 friends left over.

Patti and Jack shout, "Jump in here!"
to a child we've never even met.

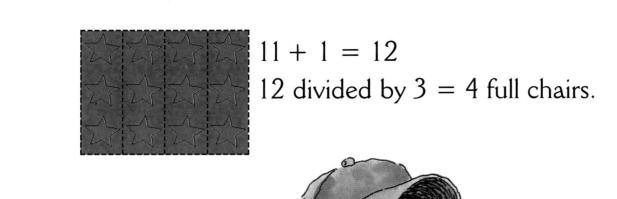

$11 + 1 = 12$

12 divided by 3 = 4 full chairs.

Then up we start. We swing to the top.

Then round and round we go!

For the Twin-Spin Cars, once more we'll divide.
The ticket man shouts, "4 people per car.
Each car must be filled before you can ride."

We can fill 2 cars,
but 3 friends are left over
from our group of 11 best friends.

4 people per car!

11 divided by 4 = 2 full cars

. . . with 3 friends left over.

Mickie, Jill and Rob scream, "Come with us!"
to a child we've never even seen.

11 + 1 = 12

12 divided by 4 = 3 full cars.

and we spin round really fast!

At last! On the raft, we don't need to divide.
There are 14 seats in all,
and every seat must be filled before we can ride.

To fill all the seats
we need to add 3 children
to our group of 11 best friends.

14 – 11 = 3 empty seats.

So we call to the child
we didn't even know,

we yell to the child
we'd never even met,

and we shout to the child
we'd never even seen before.

Then we start to slide, and to slip and slosh.

We land at the bottom

with a great big SPLASH!

Now we're 14 carnival friends!

11 + 3 = 14.

ACTIVITIES AT SCHOOL

The following activities will help you to extend children's understanding of the concepts presented in *Divide and Ride*:

• Read the story with the children and ask them to describe what is happening in each picture. Ask questions throughout the story, such as 'Which ride would you most like to go on?', 'Why?' and 'If eleven friends sit three people in each car, how many friends are left over?'

• Encourage the children to tell the story using the maths vocabulary, 'divide' and 'left over'. Introduce words such as 'groups of', 'sets of' and 'remainder'.

• Talk about familiar settings in which large groups are divided into smaller groups, such as teams for a game, rows of seats on a bus and people at each table. Make sketches or diagrams of each situation. Discuss what happens with those who are left over. Is a new team formed? Do some people have to stand on the bus? Is an additional chair added to the table?

• Draw the 11 friends using stars as shown on the maths summary pages, or use counters or pebbles to represent the friends. Together, practise grouping the friends into sets of 2s, 3s and 4s. Are there any friends left over? How many?

• Take another look at the story. What if the group of 14 new best friends went to the fairground together? How many seats would they fill on each ride? Would there be any friends left over?